Read, Trace and Write the Sight Words

a

I have a ball.

a a a a a a

I

I have a bat.

am

I am hungry.

am am am am am am

an

I want an apple.

an an an an an an

as

I sit as I eat.

as as as as as as as

at

She sat at the desk.

at at at at at at

Write the sentences with the correct words

a   I   am

an   as   at

Do ______ you are told.

He has ___ kite.

She has ____ apple.

___ sit ___ my desk.

___ ____ tired.

Write your own sentences with the words

a   I   am

an   as   at

Read, Trace and Write the Sight Words

be

I will be late.

be be be be be

by

Please sit by me.

by by by by

do

Do you like dogs?

do do do do

go

I go to sleep.

go go go go

he

He flew the kite.

he he he he he

if

He will win if he scores.

if if if if if

Write the sentences with the correct words

be	by	do
go	he	if

You can ____ it!

____ likes the kite.

Eat an apple ___ you want.

I will ____ happy.

They ____ ____ bus.

Write your own sentences with the words

be	by	do
go	he	if

Read, Trace and Write the Sight Words

in

The ducks swim in the pond.

in in in in in in

is

She is walking the dog.

is is is is is is

it

It is a koala in the tree.

it it it it it it

me

Let me go to sleep.

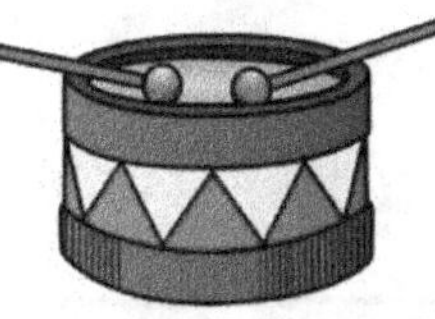

me me me me

my

Here is my drum.

my my my my

no

We have no school today.

no no no no

Write the sentences with the correct words

in   is   it
me   my   no

Please give ____ the ball.

There are ____ dogs allowed.

__ is a magic ball.

This ____ _____ desk.

The dog ____ ____ the tub.

> in   is   it
> me my no

Read, Trace and Write the Sight Words

of
It's a piece of cake.

on
The boy sat on the couch.

or
Do you like cats or dogs?

so
I am so happy today.

to
The bus went to school.

up
The jet flew up in the sky.

Write the sentences with the correct words

> of   on   or
>
> so   to   up

He got hit ___ the head.

Walk ahead ___ me.

Is that an apple ___ orange?

The giraffe is ___ tall.

It went ___ ___ the moon.

Write your own sentences with the words

of	on	or
so	to	up

Read, Trace and Write the Sight Words

us

Let us cook for you tonight.

us us us us us

we

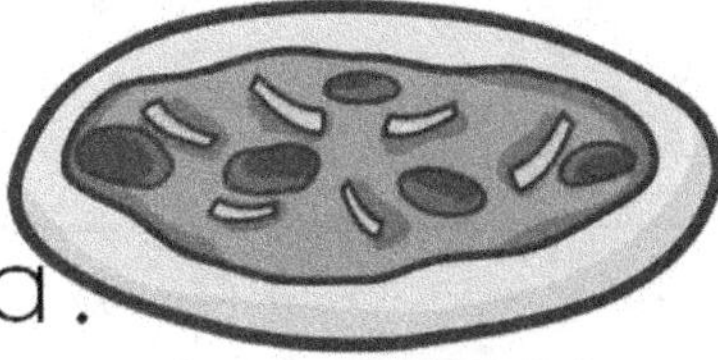

We will make a big pizza.

we we we we

air

The balloon is in the air.

air air air air

all

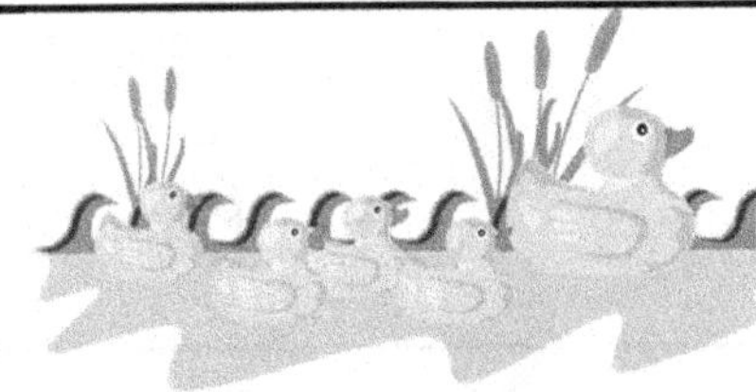

All the ducks are in a row.

all all all all

and

The wolf jumped and scored.

and and and and

any

Do you have any money?

any any any any

Write the sentences with the correct words

us   we   air
all   and   any

____ went on the sled.

I like eggs ___ bacon.

The jet flew in the ___.

I can bake at ___ time.

___ of ___ went in the car.

Write your own sentences with the words

us   we   air
all   and   any

Read, Trace and Write the Sight Words

are

Three birds are singing.

are are are are

ask

Please ask your question.

ask ask ask ask

ate

The panda ate bamboo

ate ate ate ate

bed

I sleep in the bed.

bed bed bed

big

The elephant is so big!

big big big big

box

What's in the heavy box?

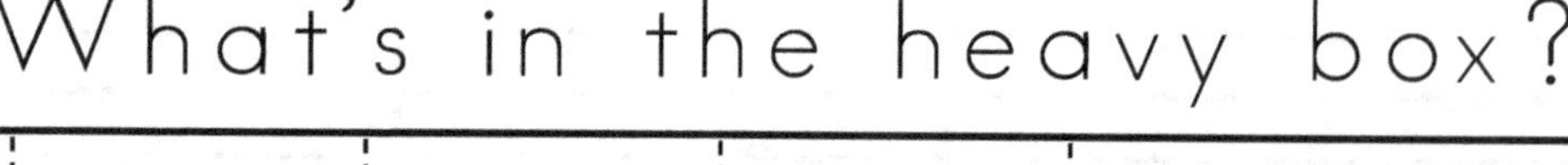
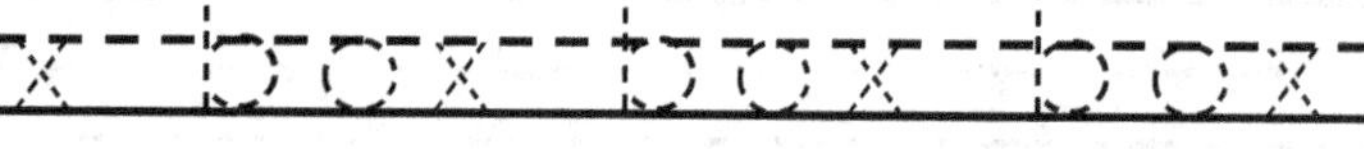

box box box box

Write the sentences with the correct words

are   ask   ate
bed   big   box

Who ____ the banana?

The cat sleeps in the ____.

Did you ____ your question?

Two dolphins ____ jumping.

He carries a ____ ____.

Write your own sentences with the words

are   ask   ate
bed   big   box

Read, Trace and Write the Sight Words

boy

The boy and girl went to school.

boy   boy   boy

but

I want to go, but I am sick.

but   but   but   but

buy

I can buy some candy.

buy   buy   buy

can

She can jump rope.

can   can   can

car

He drove the car fast.

car   car   car

cat

My cat is very hungry.

car   car   cat

Write the sentences with the correct words

boy   but   buy

can   car   cat

He will ____ ice cream.  

He used the paint in the ____. 

A tiger is a big ____. 

The mouse is small, ____ strong. 

The ____ will drive the ____. 

Write your own sentences with the words

> boy   but   buy
> can   car   cat

Read, Trace and Write the Sight Words

cow
The cow likes to eat grass.

cow cow cow

day
Today is a good day for me!

day day day

did
Did you sleep well last night?

did did did did

dog
The girl walks the dog outside.

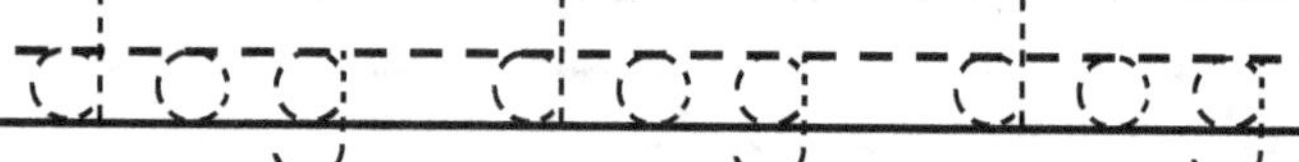

dog dog dog

eat
Panda bears eat bamboo.

eat eat eat

egg
What's coming out of the egg?

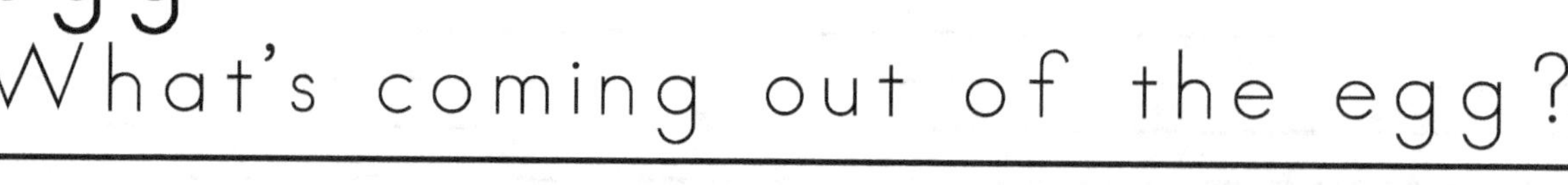

egg egg egg

Write the sentences with the correct words

| cow | day | did |
| dog | eat | egg |

I dropped an ________.

Do you like to _____ ice cream?

I don't see the ____ here.

Tomorrow will be a new _____.

_____ you walk the ____ today?

Write your own sentences with the words

cow   day   did
dog   eat   egg

Read, Trace and Write the Sight Words

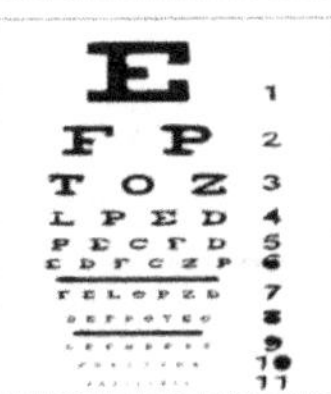

end

How will the book end?

end end end

eye

I have to go to the eye doctor.

eye eye eye

fly

We will fly in the plane.

fly fly fly

for

It's time for bed now.

for for for

get

Get a pencil and paper ready.

get get get

has

She has a test today at school.

has has has

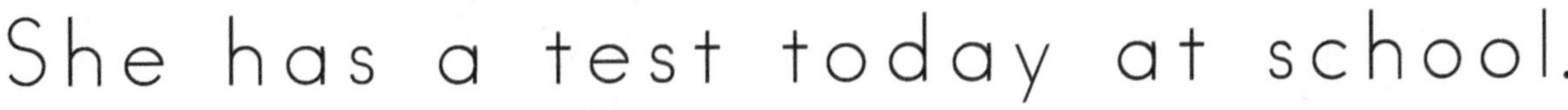

Write the sentences with the correct words

end	eye	fly
for	get	had

She made a cake _____ me.

I waited at the ____.

I ___ to stay in bed.

Something is in my ______.

Please ___ the ____ out!

Write your own sentences with the words

end   eye   fly
for   get   had

Read, Trace and Write the Sight Words

has

He has a yellow soccer ball.

has has has

her

She walks her dog everyday.

her her her

him

She walked to school with him.

him him him

his

His magic show was good.

his his his

how

How do magnets work?

how how how

its

The cat wants its food.

its its its

Write the sentences with the correct words

has   her   him
his   how   its

She sat at ____ desk.

He ____ a fast car.

The dog took ____ bath.

The water balloon hit ____.

____ was ____ magic show?

Write your own sentences with the words

has   her   him
his   how   its

Read, Trace and Write the Sight Words

leg
The caterpillar hurts its leg.

leg   leg   leg

let
Let me go to sleep.

let   let   let

man
The man painted the room.

man   man   man

may
May I read my book now?

may   may   may

men
Three wise men came.

men   men   men

new
The dog has a new car.

new   new   new

Write the sentences with the correct words

> leg   let   man
>
> may   men   new

I ____ him drive my car.

Those two ____ are friends.

____ I have some food?

I played my ____ drum.

The ____ broke his ____.

Write your own sentences with the words

leg   let   man
may   men   new

Read, Trace and Write the Sight Words

not
That animal is not a dog.

not not not

now
Now is the time for lunch.

now now now

off
The plane took off into the sky.

off off off

old
The old man likes butterflies.

old old old

one
I can buy one ice cream.

one one one

our
We walked to our house.

our our our

Write the sentences with the correct words

not	now	off
old	one	our

Here is a very ____ car.

Please take _____ your shoes.

I have ___ red apple.

This is ___ school.

____ is ___ the time to sleep.  

Write your own sentences with the words

not	now	off
old	one	our

Read, Trace and Write the Sight Words

out
The dolphin jumped out of the water.

out out out

pig
I saw a cute pig.

pig pig pig

put
We put out the fire with water.

put put put

ran
The girl ran to Grandma's house.

ran ran ran

red
They rode a red sled down.

red red red

run
The man likes to run for exercise.

run run run

Write the sentences with the correct words

| out | pig | put |
| ran | red | run |

_____ on your coat please.

My dog likes to _____.

That's not a ____.

You can't go ___ like that!

The ____ car ____ out of gas.

Write your own sentences with the words

| out | pig | put |
| ran | red | run |

Read, Trace and Write the Sight Words

saw

My dad can use a saw to cut wood.

saw saw saw

say

What did the boy say?

say say say

see

Do you see the bird in the tree?

see see see

set

It's time to set the table.

set set set

she

She is ready for class to begin.

she she she

sit

They all sit and listen to her.

sit sit sit

Write the sentences with the correct words

| saw | say | see |
| set | she | sit |

Please ____ the alarm for six.

Did you ____ my magic show?

Excuse me, what did you _____?

Yesterday, I ____ the game.

____ will ____ in the chair.

Write your own sentences with the words

saw   say   see

set   she   sit

Read, Trace and Write the Sight Words

sun
The sun is shining bright.

sun sun sun

the
The bee is flying to the flower.

the the the

too
I ate too much pizza.

too too too

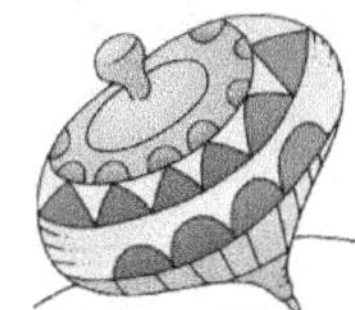

top
I spun the top on the floor.

top top top

toy
My sister's toy bear is cute.

toy toy toy

try
I will try my hardest.

try try try

Write the sentences with the correct words

| sun | the | too |
| top | toy | try |

The ___ is hot.

I got a ___ plane

I ___ to do my best.

I placed my book on ___.

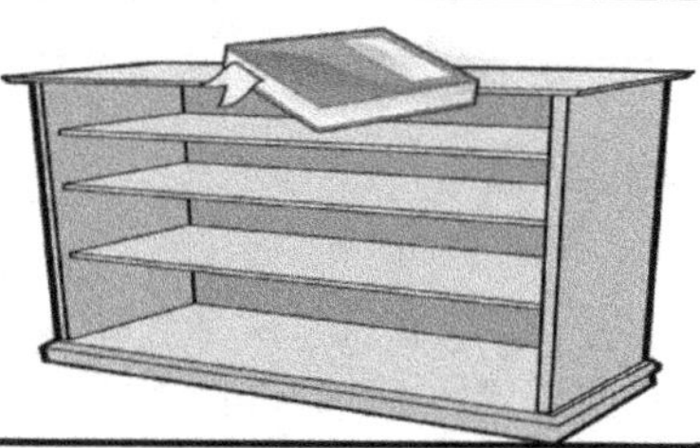

I loves apples ___!

Write your own sentences with the words

sun	the	too
top	toy	try

Read, Trace and Write the Sight Words

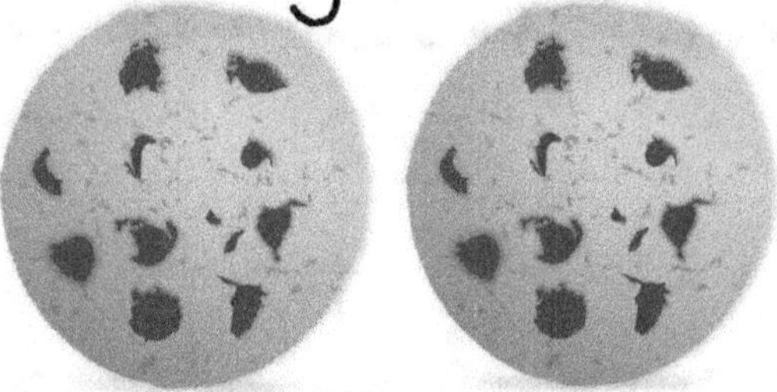

two

I have two cookies

two two two

use

I use my crayons to color.

use use use

was

He was flying a plane.

was was was

way

I found the way out!

way way way

who

Who raised their hand?.

who who who

why

Why is he crying?.

why why why

Write the sentences with the correct words

two	use	was
way	who	why

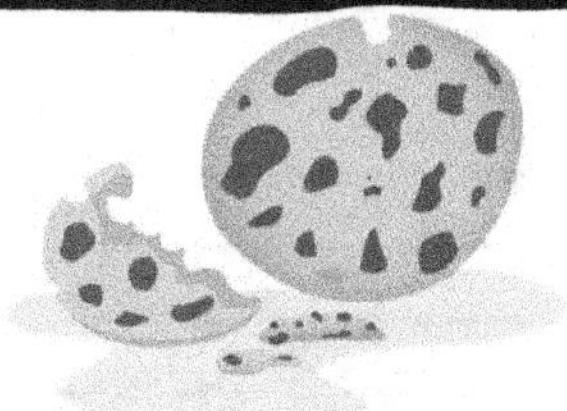

_____ ate the cookies?

I have _____ sisters.

I _____ my pencil.

_____ did you leave school?

_____ this the _____ out?

Write your own sentences with the words

two   use   was

way   who   why

Read, Trace and Write the Sight Words

yes

I said, "yes" to my mother.

yes yes yes

you

Do you have a book?.

you you you

also

I also have dancing lessons.

also also also

away

I am going away on vacation.

away away away

baby

The baby was crying.

baby baby baby

back

Don't worry, I have your back.

back back back

Write the sentences with the correct words

> yes   you   also
> away   baby   back

Did you say yes or no?

My mom is having a _____.

The bird flew ___.

My _____ stings.

____ _____ have to write.

yes   you   also
away   baby   back

Read, Trace and Write the Sight Words

ball
The cat chased the ball.
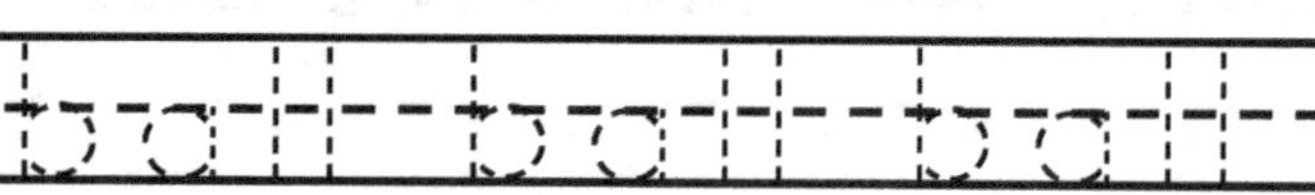

ball ball ball

bear
I saw a bear with her cub.

bear bear bear

been
I have been to Florida before.

been been been

bell
The fireman rang the bell.

bell bell bell

best
She is the best student in my class.

best best best

bird
My cat likes to watch the bird.

bird bird bird

Write the sentences with the correct words

| ball | bear | been |
| bell | best | bird |

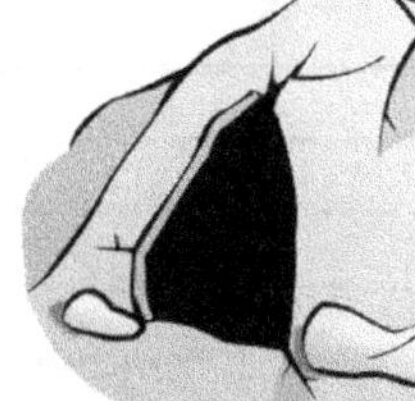

The ____ went in the cave.

The ____ rang for school.

I have ____ busy.

The ____ is in the cage.

He's the ____ at hitting a ___.

Write your own sentences with the words

ball   bear   been
bell   best   bird

Read, Trace and Write the Sight Words

blue

I found a blue butterfly.

blue blue blue

boat

We rowed the boat to land.

boat boat boat

both

We both left for school.

both both both

cake

I love to eat cake for dessert.

cake cake cake

call

The teacher will call on me.

call call call

came

I came home on the bus.

came came came

Write the sentences with the correct words

blue   boat   both
cake   call   came

She made a ____ for me.

She _____ alone.

The ___ was on water.

____ an ambulance.

We ____ like the color _____.

Write your own sentences with the words

blue   boat   both

cake   call   came

Read, Trace and Write the Sight Words

coat

The bear has a nice warm coat.

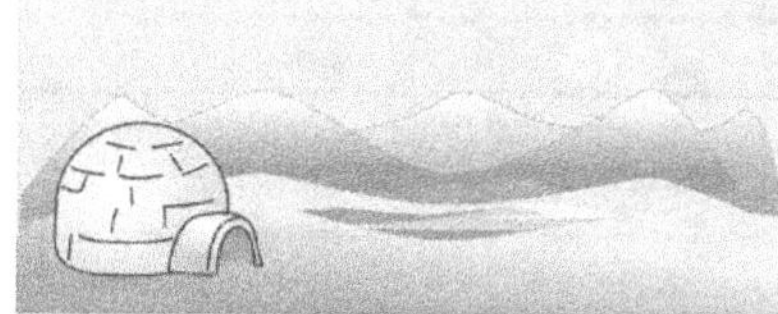

cold

It is cold in the Arctic.

come

Where did this money come from?

corn

He eats corn flakes at breakfast.

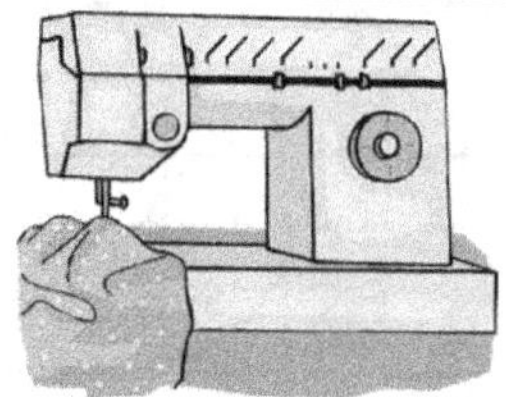

does

How does this machine work?

doll

I have a favorite doll..

Write the sentences with the correct words

coat   cold   come

corn   does   doll

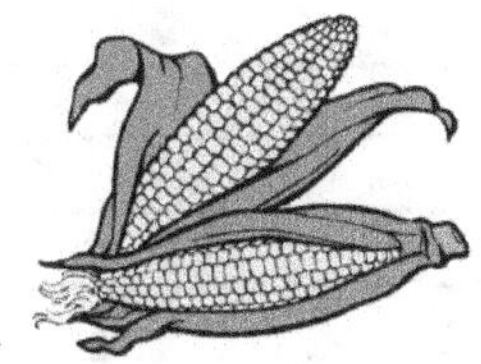

This ___ is fresh.

She ___ her homework.

I love my ___.

___ visit us soon!

It's ___, so put a ___ on

coat   cold   come
corn   does   doll

Read, Trace and Write the Sight Words

door

Please open the door.

---

door door door

---

down

The beaver chopped the tree down.

---

down down down

---

duck

I fed the duck some bread.

---

duck duck duck

---

each

We each get one piece.

---

each each each

---

even

Two is an even number..

---

even even even

---

farm

I live on a farm.

---

farm farm farm

Write the sentences with the correct words

| door | down | duck |
| each | even | farm |

Sloths hangs upside ____.

Sheep live on the ___.

I quacked like a ____.

I open the ____.

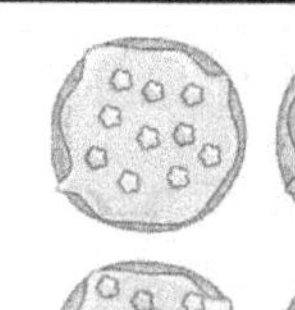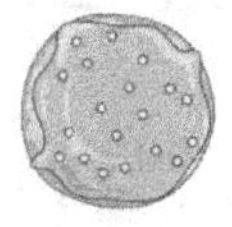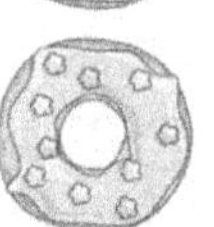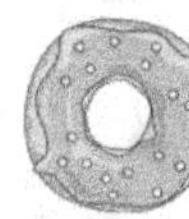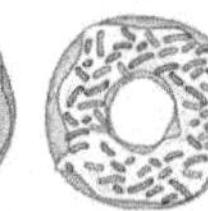

We ____ got an ____ amount.

Write your own sentences with the words

door   down   duck
each   even   farm

Read, Trace and Write the Sight Words

fast

The car went fast.

fast fast fast

feet

His feet were bare.

feet feet feet

find

I will find you.

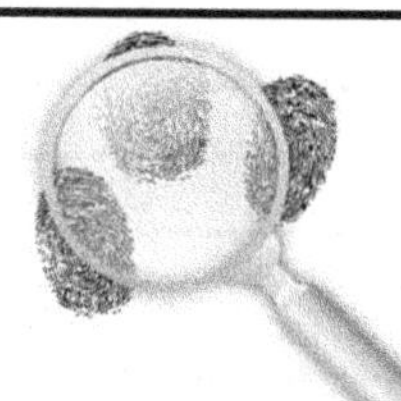

find find find

fire

We made a fire to cook.

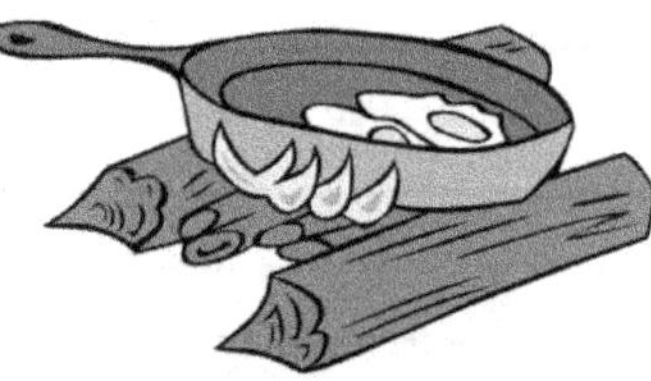

fire fire fire

fish

I have a pet fish.

fish fish fish

five

I have five cookies.

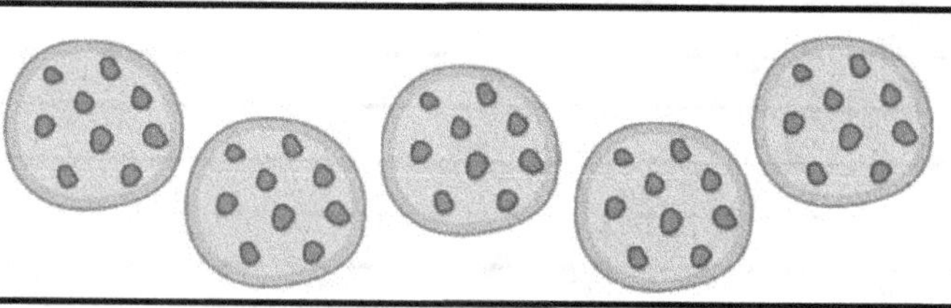

five five five

Write the sentences with the correct words

fast   feet   find
fire   fish   five

Is the ____ warm enough?

My ____ are so tired.

The flower has ____ petals.

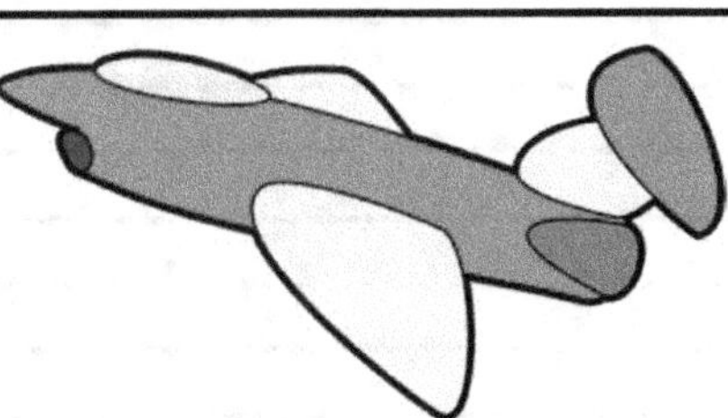

The red jet flew ____.

Can you ____ the ____?

Write your own sentences with the words

fast   feet   find
fire   fish   five

Read, Trace and Write the Sight Words

form
Please form a line behind her.

form form form

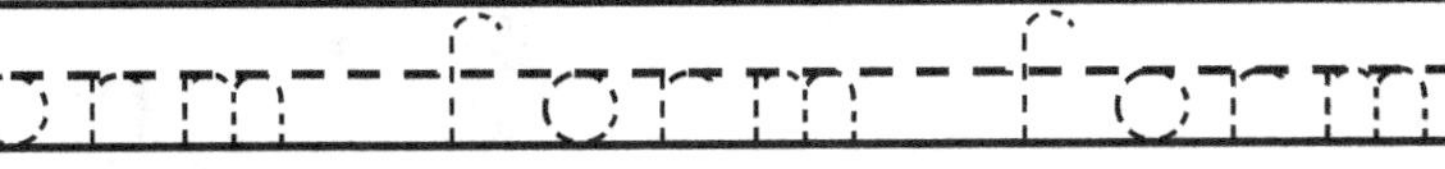

four
Have you seen a four-leaf clover?

four four four

from
He jumped from the boat.

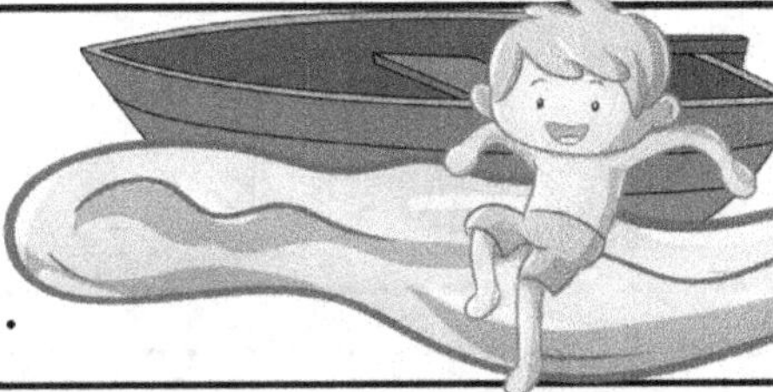

from from from

game
Let's play a game of basketball.

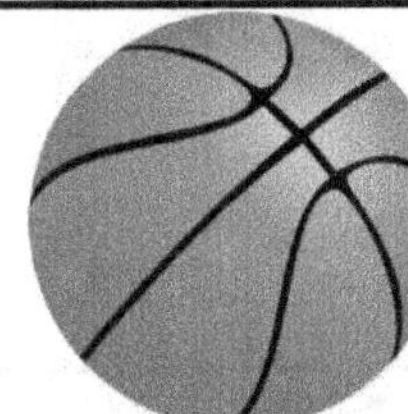

game game game

gave
Dad gave Mom a present.

gave gave gave

girl
The girl carries three books.

girl girl girl

Write the sentences with the correct words

form   four   from
game   gave   girl

I like this card ____.

We walk ____ here.

Mom filled out the ____.

The ____ likes to dance.

I ____ her ____ quarters.

Write your own sentences with the words

form   four   from

game   gave   girl

Read, Trace and Write the Sight Words

give
Can you please give me glue?

give give give

goes
He goes to school today

goes goes goes

good
Both of my dogs are very good.

good good good

hand
He shook her hand when they met.

hand hand hand

have
Do you have an eraser?

have have have

head
She wore a crown on her head.

head head head

Write the sentences with the correct words

give	goes	good
hand	have	head

I have a banana.

Never ____ up!

Please ____ in your test.

What ____ in your backpack?

I have a ____ ____ for math.

give   goes   good
hand   have   head

Read, Trace and Write the Sight Words

help
They called an ambulance for help.

help help help

here
Here is where we are on the map.

here here here

hill
A lighthouse sits upon the hill.

hill hill hill

home
This cave is the bear's home.

home home home

into
The animals went into the boat.

into into into

jump
Kangaroos like to jump far.

jump jump jump

Write the sentences with the correct words

> help   here   hill
> home   into   jump

The king lives ____.

Can you ____ me?

This is our ____.

They walked up the ____.

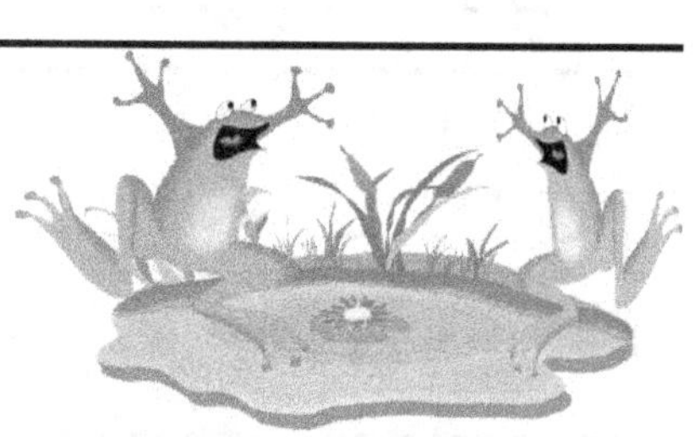

Frogs ____ ____ the water.

Write your own sentences with the words

| help | here | hill |
| home | into | jump |

Read, Trace and Write the Sight Words

just

Can you read just one more story?

just just just

kind 

The nurse was very kind to help me.

kind kind kind

know 

Do you know where the library is?

know know know

land

Someday we may land on Mars.

land land land

like 

My brother doesn't like dogs.

like like like

line 

Write your name on the line.

line line line

Write the sentences with the correct words

| just | kind | know |
| land | like | line |

We stood in ____.

The train ____ left.

The plan will ____ soon.

I ____ how to read.

I ____ this ____ of candy

Write your own sentences with the words

just   kind   know
land   like   line

Read, Trace and Write the Sight Words

live
Where do monkeys live?

long
He has a long way to travel.

look
He will look closely for clues.

made
The chef made a pizza for us.

make
Make a circle with your pencil.

many
Many animals live in the sea.

Write the sentences with the correct words

live   long   look
made   make   many

Can you ____ a vase from clay?

Fish must ____ in the water.

She ____ a birthday cake for me.

We went for a ____ walk in the woods.

____ at how ____ shells I have found!

Write your own sentences with the words

live   long   look
made   make   many

Read, Trace and Write the Sight Words

milk
I drink milk at every lunch.

milk milk milk

more
Can I play more video games?

more more more

most
Who got the most awards?

most most most

move
Look how fast that snail can move!

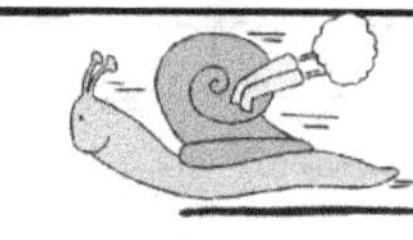

move move move

much
The panda has too much to eat.

much much much

must
She must not be late for work.

must must must

Write the sentences with the correct words

milk   more   most
move   much   must

Please ____ your chair to make room.

I ____ study for the spelling test.

It's not ____, but it's all I have.

Can I have ____ food please?

This cow give the ____ ____ of all.

Write your own sentences with the words

live long look
made make many

Read, Trace and Write the Sight Words

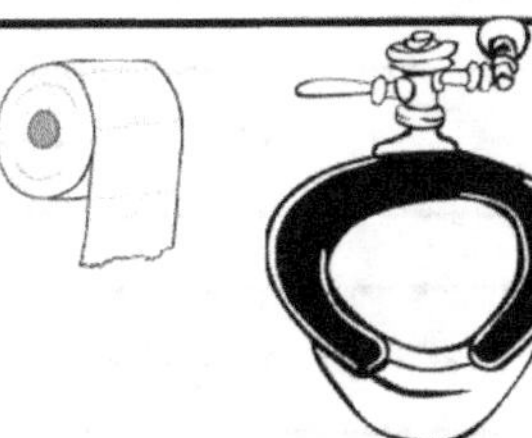

name

I write my name on all my papers.

name name name

need

I need to go to the bathroom.

need need need

nest

The pelican made a huge nest.

nest nest nest

once

Once upon a time there was a frog.

once once once

only

I have only one pen for school.

only only only

open

Can you please open my milk?

open open open

Write the sentences with the correct words

name   need   nest
once   only   open

He has his hair cut ____ a month.

Can you please ___ the door for me?

She ____ drinks water for dinner.

Can you write your ___ on the paper?

Birds ___ a ___ to lay their eggs.

Write your own sentences with the words

name   need   nest
once   only   open

Read, Trace and Write the Sight Words

over

The cow jumped over the moon.

over over over

page

She read a page from the book.

page page page

part

The robot is missing a part.

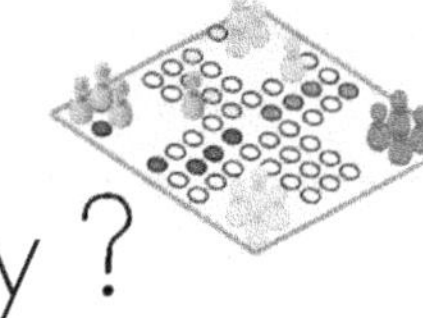

part part part

play

What game do you want to play?

play play play

pull

Look at the train pull the load.

pull pull pull

rain

She had an umbrella for the rain.

rain rain rain

Write the sentences with the correct words

over   page   part
play   pull   rain

They climbed ____ the hill.

In the book, what ____ are we on?

We had to ____ the sled up the hill.

The ___ made the grass grow tall.

I have the main ____ in the ____.

Write your own sentences with the words

over   page   part
play   pull   rain

Read, Trace and Write the Sight Words

read

She likes to read a lot of books.

read read

ride

Do you know how to ride a bicycle?

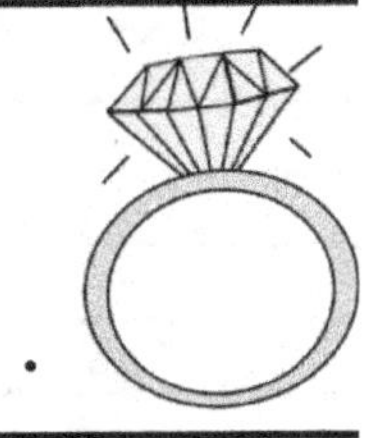

ride ride

ring

My dad gave my mom a new ring.

ring ring

said

He said it was time to go.

said said

same

Don't put all your eggs in the same basket.

same same

seed

The plant grew from a small seed.

seed seed

Write the sentences with the correct words

read　　ride　　ring
said　　same　　seed

He planted a bean ____ in the garden.

I ____ "good-bye" to my friends.

They made a ____ around the fire.

Tomorrow I will ____ the horse.

I think we ____ the ____ book.

read	ride	ring
said	same	seed

Read, Trace and Write the Sight Words

shoe

Have you seen my missing shoe.

shoe shoe

show

He put on a magic show for us.

show show

sing

I can hear the bird sing loudly.

sing sing

snow

Playing in the snow is so much fun.

snow snow

some

At Thanksgiving, we ate some pie.

some some

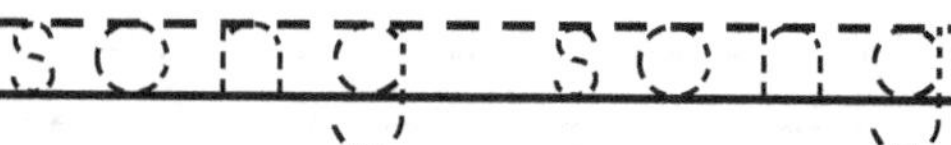

song

I heard my favorite song on the radio.

song song

Write the sentences with the correct words

shoe   show   sing

snow   some   song

Can I have ____ orange juice please?

There is a ____ under your bed.

We will go sledding in the ____.

Tonight, at seven is the talent ____.

They will ____ a ____ together.

Write your own sentences with the words

shoe   show   sing

snow   some   song

Read, Trace and Write the Sight Words

soon

Soon it will be time to wake up.

stop

Stop before crossing the street.

such

This is such good music.

take

He will take the dog for a walk.

tell

Can you tell what time it is?

than

The rabbit is faster than the turtle.

Write the sentences with the correct words

soon   stop   such
take   tell   than

Can you ____ a picture of me?

I will ____ you about the story I read.

You should not be in ____ a hurry.

The sloth is slower ____ the cheetah.

____ I will have to ____ swimming.

Write your own sentences with the words

soon   stop   such
take   tell   than

Read, Trace and Write the Sight Words

that

What is that loud sound?

that that

them

My family went to visit them.

them them

then

Let's do our homework, then play.

then then

they

Yesterday, they all went swimming.

they they

this

This is my favorite video game.

this this

time

It's time to go to Spanish class.

time time

Write the sentences with the correct words

| that | them | then |
| they | this | time |

____ all held hands in a circle.

First crack the egg, ____ mix it.

He gave gifts to all of ____.

What ____ is breakfast this morning?

Should I use ____ hat or ____ cap?

Write your own sentences with the words

that them then
they this time

Read, Trace and Write the Sight Words

tree
We have a big tree in our yard.

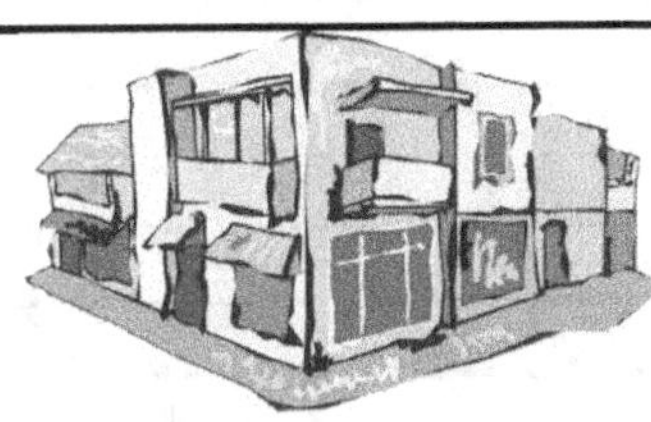

tree tree

turn
Turn left at the corner.

turn turn

upon
Once upon a time there was a queen.

upon upon

very
The chicks are very hungry.

very very

walk
We will walk to the bookstore.

walk walk

want
Do you want ice cream?

want want

Write the sentences with the correct words

tree	turn	upon
very	walk	want

What do you ____ to eat for lunch?

The boys went for a ____ in the park.

Please ____ in your paper.

In summer, it's ____ hot.

The bird sits ____ the ____ branch.

Write your own sentences with the words

| tree | turn | upon |
| very | walk | want |

Read, Trace and Write the Sight Words

wash

It's time to wash the smelly dog.

wash wash

well

They used to get water from a well.

well well

went

This pig went to the market.

went went

were

I wish I were an astronaut in space.

were were

what

What food is healthy to eat?

what what

when

When does winter break start?

when when

Write the sentences with the correct words

wash   well   went
were   what   when

____ time is your favorite show?

_____ do we need to go to the doctor?

They ___ going to the movies tonight.

Tonight, I need to ___ my hair.

After practice, the play ____ very ___.

wash   well   went
were   what   when

Read, Trace and Write the Sight Words

will

Will you please help with my reading?

will will

wind

Today the wind is blowing hard.

wind wind

wish

He made a wish with the lamp.

wish wish

with

I'm going with my friend.

with with

wood

My dad can make it from wood.

wood wood

work

The fox is ready to go to work.

work work

Write the sentences with the correct words

will   wind   wish
with   wood   work

He likes to eat jam ___ his toast.

On her birthday, the girl made a ___.

The ___ pushed my kite up higher.

The man bought ___ to make repairs.

Which day ___ ___ for you to come?

will   wind   wish
with   wood   work

Read, Trace and Write the Sight Words

your
Excuse me, what's your name?

your your

about
He talked about his plane trip.

about about

after
After spelling we have science.

after after

again
Could you repeat the directions again.

again again

apple
An apple is a very healthy food.

apple apple

black
Penguins are black and white.

black black

Write the sentences with the correct words

your	about	after
again	apple	black

The boy's hair was dark _____.

I like to eat a red ____ for lunch.

Can I borrow ____ pencil please?

I wrote all ____ my family.

___ I practice, I will try ____.

Write your own sentences with the words

your	about	after
again	apple	black

Read, Trace and Write the Sight Words

bread

I just need bread and cheese.

bread bread

brown

The brown squirrel ran away.

brown brown

chair

The bear sat in the rocking chair.

chair chair

could

I could answer the question.

could could

don't

I don't think the robot works.

don't don't

every

Every day I like to read my book.

every every

Write the sentences with the correct words

| bread | brown | chair |
| could | don't | every |

My mom bought ___ and milk.

I ____ like to eat my vegetables.

I ___ ride a bike by myself last year.

____ morning, my dad walks the dog.

My dad likes to sit in the ____ ____.

Write your own sentences with the words

bread	brown	chair
could	don't	every

Read, Trace and Write the Sight Words

first
I won first place in the science fair.

first first

floor
The floor was dirty, so she mopped.

floor floor

found
Have you found my wallet?

found found

funny
I laughed at the funny joke.

funny funny

going
She is going to the store today.

going going

grass
Cows like to eat grass outside.

grass grass

Write the sentences with the correct words

first   floor   found
funny   going   grass

Dad mows the ___ on Saturday.

___ we do reading, then we do math.

The eggs fell to the ___ and cracked.

Mom is ___ to the bank to get money.

I ___ the clown to be very ___.

Write your own sentences with the words

first floor found
funny going grass

Read, Trace and Write the Sight Words

great

I got an award for such a great job.

great great

green

The tree is full of green leaves.

green green

horse

The horse lives in the red barn.

horse horse

house

Welcome back to my house.

house house

kitty

My kitty needs more food.

kitty kitty

large

Blue whales are very large.

large large

Write the sentences with the correct words

> great   green   horse
> house   kitty   large

I have a ___ thumb for growing plants.

I think I did ____ on the test today.

We got a new ___ for a pet.

The cowboy rode a ___ on the trail.

That family lives in quite a _____ ______.

Write your own sentences with the words

great green horse
house kitty large

Read, Trace and Write the Sight Words

learn

Can old dogs learn new tricks?

learn learn

means

I don't know what that word means.

means means

money

He saved his money in his bank.

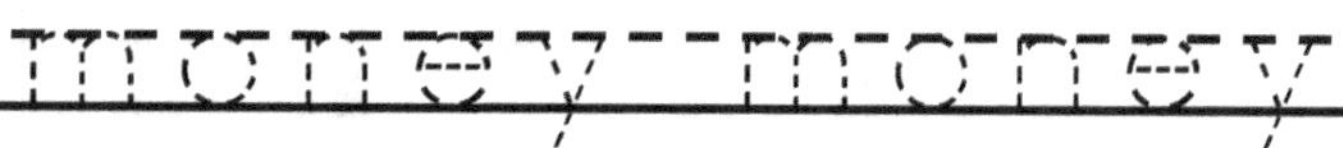

night

At night it gets dark and cold.

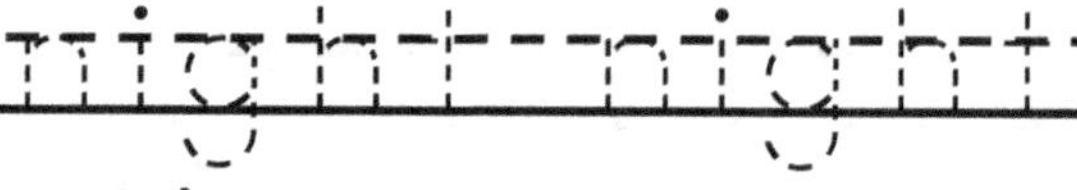

other

My parents really love each other.

other other

paper

Who flew a paper airplane in class?

Write the sentences with the correct words

> learn   means   money
> night   other   paper

At ____, the moon and stars come out.

When can we see each ____ again?

Do you know what that word _____?

I like to ____ about science and math.

____ is made from _____.

Write your own sentences with the words

learn   means   money
night   other   paper

Read, Trace and Write the Sight Words

party

Children swam at the pool party.

party party

place

This is the place where we ate lunch.

place place

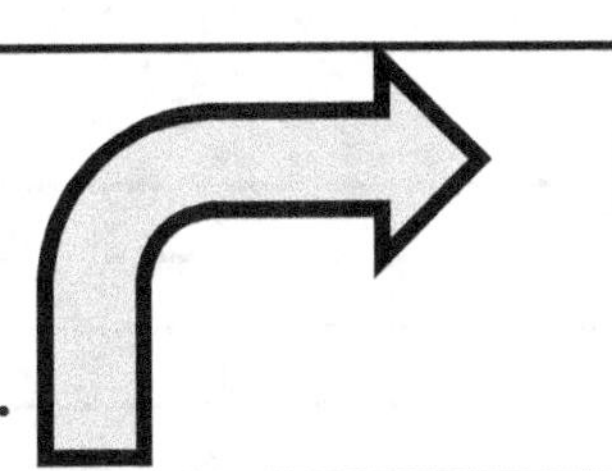

point

My pencil has a sharp point.

point point

right

Turn right at the stop sign.

right right

robin

I saw a robin building a nest

robin robin

round

In math, we learned how to round.

round round

Write the sentences with the correct words

party	place	point
right	robin	round

What is the ____ of the story?

The kids enjoyed the birthday ____.

The ___ laid eggs in the nest.

The moon is bright and ____ tonight.

Can you ____ the books the ____ way?

Write your own sentences with the words

party	place	point
right	robin	round

Read, Trace and Write the Sight Words

sheep

I counted sheep to fall asleep.

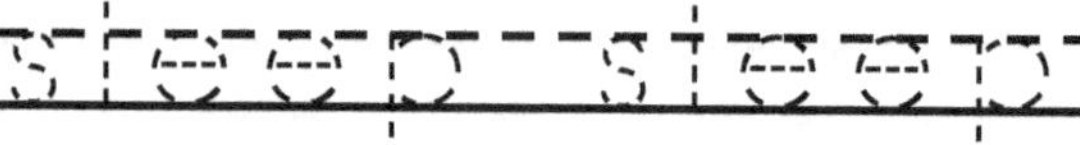

sleep

I went to sleep at eight o'clock.

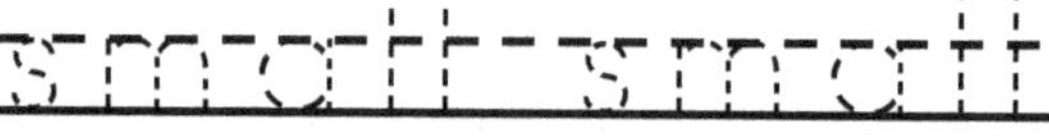

small

The small ant crawled on the floor.

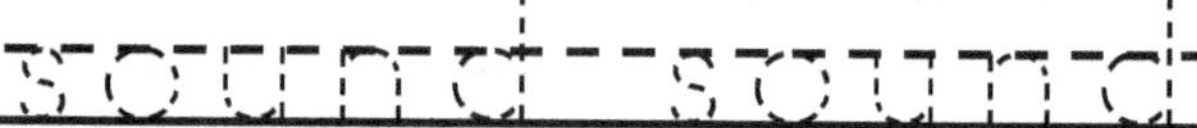

sound

At the sound of the bell, you can go.

spell

I can spell the word "giraffe".

stick

The kids hit the piñata with a stick.

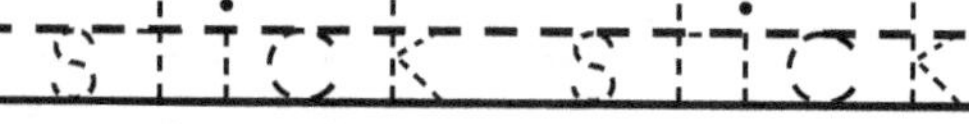

Write the sentences with the correct words

sheep	sleep	small
sound	spell	stick

The boy hit the ball with the ___.

The button was so ___ I couldn't see it.

Can you ___ your teacher's name?

When we visited the farm, we saw ___.

I can't ___ with all this ___ tonight.

Write your own sentences with the words

| sheep | sleep | small |
| sound | spell | stick |

Read, Trace and Write the Sight Words

still
Is the baby still sleeping?

still still

study
I have to study for school.

study study

table
Please set the table for dinner.

table table

thank
Thank you for the gift you gave me.

thank thank

their
Tonight, we went to their house.

their their

there
There are many fish in the sea.

there there

Write the sentences with the correct words

| still | study | table |
| thank | their | there |

His black bookbag is right over ____.

At night, we eat dinner at the ______.

____ you for all your help yesterday.

I should ___ for the next spelling test.

They ___ cannot find ___ missing socks.

Write your own sentences with the words

| still | study | table |
| thank | their | there |

Read, Trace and Write the Sight Words

these

These scissors cut very well.

these these

thing

What do you call that old thing?

thing thing

think

He had to think about the problem.

think think

those

Those are my sunglasses.

those those

three

Once there were three pigs.

three three

under

The submarine goes under the sea.

under under

Write the sentences with the correct words

these	thing	think
those	three	under

My friend always says the same ____.

I always eat ____ meals everyday.

____ are my books on the table there.

____ flowers are pretty, aren't they?

I ____ your book is ____ the chair.

Write your own sentences with the words

these	thing	think
those	three	under

Read, Trace and Write the Sight Words

watch
My cat loves to watch the fish.

water
Turtles like to live near the water.

where
Where can we find the treasure?

which
Which house do you live in?

white
Pandas are black and white.

words
She has read a lot of words.

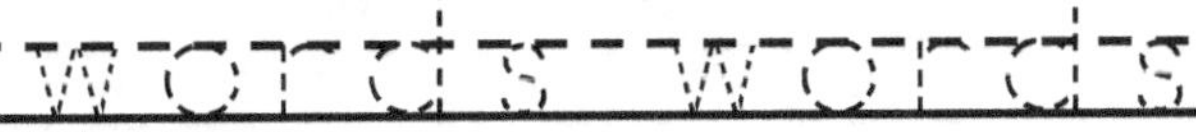

Write the sentences with the correct words

watch   water   where
which   white   words

My grandfather has ____ hair.

I use my ____ to know the time.

I read all the ____ in the book.

____ came first, the chicken or the egg?

____ did all the ____ in the pool go?

Write your own sentences with the words

watch	water	where
which	white	words

Read, Trace and Write the Sight Words

world

Many people live around the world.

world world

would

I wish you would listen to me.

would would

write

I will write a letter to grandma.

write write

years

Right now, I am seven years old.

years years

always

My parents will always love me.

always always

animal

The sloth is the slowest animal.

animal animal

Write the sentences with the correct words

world   would   write
years   always   animal

I _____ do my homework on time.

I will drive a car in nine ______.

The ___ is a very big place.

The cheetah is the fastest ____.

I ____ ____ a letter, if I could.

Write your own sentences with the words

world   would   write
years   always   animal

Read, Trace and Write the Sight Words

answer

Can you answer the phone?

answer answer

around

My cat jumps around the house.

around around

before

I brushed my teeth before bed.

before before

called

The man called his friend.

called called

change

The tadpole will change into a frog.

change change

farmer

The farmer drove a red tractor.

farmer farmer

Write the sentences with the correct words

answer	around	before
called	change	farmer

I went to ____ for bedtime.

My dog ran quickly ____ the house.

Can you ____ the question?

The ____ milked the cows.

Please, do not speak ____ you are ____.

Write your own sentences with the words

answer around before
called change farmer

Read, Trace and Write the Sight Words

father

My father was so proud of me.

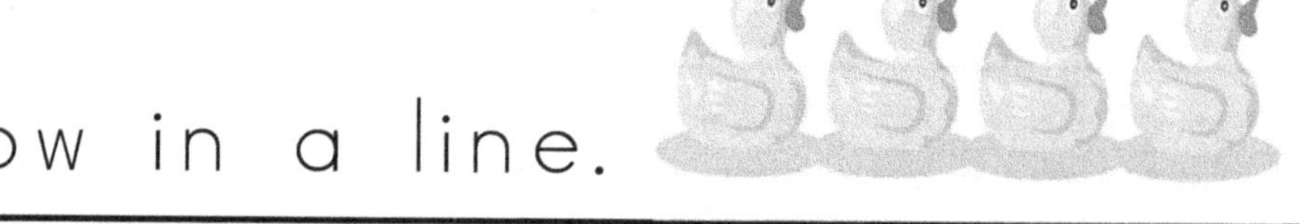

father father

flower

I gave my mom a pink flower.

flower flower

follow

The ducks follow in a line.

follow follow

garden

My mom loves to garden.

garden garden

ground

The acorn fell to the ground.

ground ground

letter

What letter comes next?

letter letter

Write the sentences with the correct words

| father | flower | follow |
| garden | ground | letter |

Can you _____ me through the maze?

Roses are my favorite _____.

I mailed a _____ at the post office.

I dropped my money on the _____.

My _____ grew corn in our _____.

Write your own sentences with the words

father   flower   follow
garden   ground   letter

Read, Trace and Write the Sight Words

little
My cat found a little mouse.

little little

mother
The mother walked with her baby.
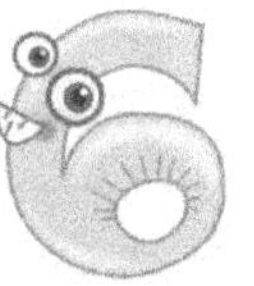

mother mother

number
What number comes after six?
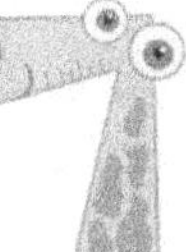

number number

people
Many people live around the world.
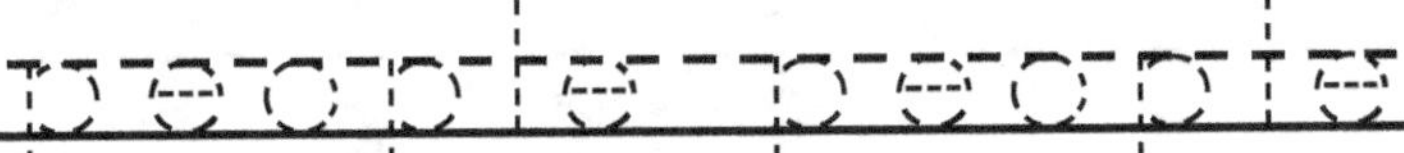

people people

please
Please close the door.

please please

pretty
The colorful butterfly is pretty.

pretty pretty
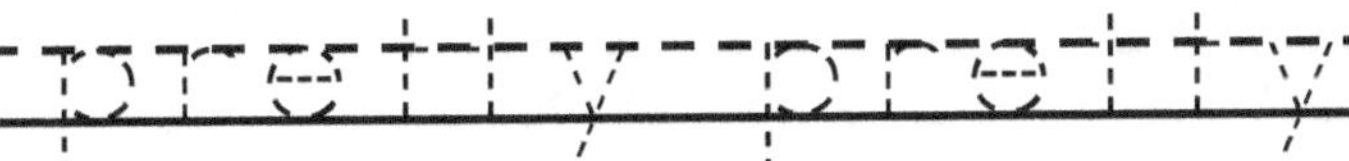

Write the sentences with the correct words

little   mother   number
people   please   pretty

When I was ____ I could not read.

______ your paper one to ten.

The food tasted ______ good.

I saw many ______ in the park today.

____ listen to your ______ and father.

Write your own sentences with the words

little   mother   number
people   please   pretty

Read, Trace and Write the Sight Words

rabbit

The rabbit likes to eat carrots. 

rabbit rabbit

school

We go to a big school. 

school school

should

You should be nice to your sister. 

should should

sister

He painted eggs with his sister. 

sister sister

street

This street has many tall houses. 

street street

things

All my things are on the bookcase.

things things

Write the sentences with the correct words

rabbit   school   should
sister   street   things

I like to play games with my _____.

My mom went through a box of ____.

You _____ listen to your parents.

When I was young, I had a pet _____.

My _______ is down this _______.

Write your own sentences with the words

rabbit	school	should
sister	street	things

Read, Trace and Write the Sight Words

window
I saw houses through the window. 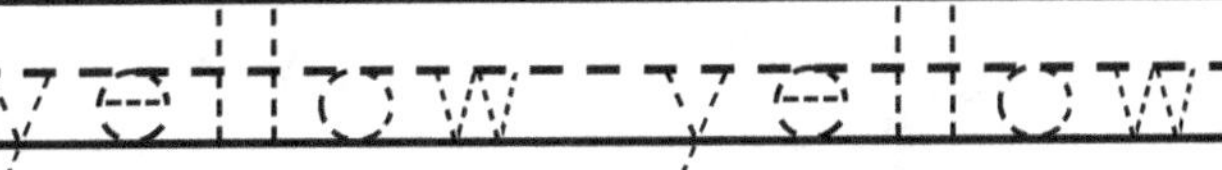

window window

yellow
A yellow bus zoomed by us.

yellow yellow

America
I live in the United States of America.

America America

another
Would you like another orange juice?

another another

because
He couldn't come, because he's sick.

because because

brother
She went sailing with her brother. 

brother brother

Write the sentences with the correct words

window	yellow	America
another	because	brother

I moved from Canada to ________.

My _____ always teases me.

May I please have _______ cookie?

I didn't go to school, ______ I'm sick.

I saw a _____ bus through the _______.

Write your own sentences with the words

window   yellow   America
another   because   brother

Read, Trace and Write the Sight Words

chicken 

I saw a chicken on the farm. 

chicken chicken

morning 

In the morning I eat breakfast.

morning morning

picture 

My dad's picture is on the wall.

picture picture

through 

The dog jumped through the hoop.

through through

sentence 

I can read the first sentence.

sentence sentence

different 

These animals are different.

different different

Write the sentences with the correct words

| chicken | morning | picture |
| through | sentence | different |

Can you find the __________ of me?

I eat eggs and ham in the __________.

Our __________ gives us eggs to eat.

I went __________ the park.

Can you write a __________ __________?

Write your own sentences with the words

chicken   morning   picture
through   sentence   different

www.ingramcontent.com/pod-product-compliance
Lightning Source LLC
Chambersburg PA
CBHW080738120726
48001CB00009B/2623